Grace

CO-DKL-116

Kay Gardiner and Ann Shayne

INTRODUCTION

St st:	Stockinette stitch
St(s):	Stitch(es)
Tbl:	Through the back loop(s)
Tog:	Together
WS:	Wrong side
W&t:	Wrap and turn. On a RS row, move yarn to the front of work, slip next stitch, take yarn to the back of work, slip wrapped stitch to left needle. Turn work. On a WS row, move yarn to the back of work, slip next stitch, bring yarn to the front of work, slip wrapped stitch back to left needle, turn work.
Wyif:	With yarn in front
Yo:	Yarnover

J OJI LOCATELLI first burst onto the knitting stage in 2010 with the online publication of an elegantly engineered cardigan. It had cascading fronts and a dramatic flared silhouette, and she modeled it herself, standing in front of a wrought iron gate, wearing jeans. This was not a tentative toe-dip into knitwear design. Joji went for her vision of the cardigan she'd wanted to knit but couldn't find a pattern for—and knitters everywhere loved it.

In the more than a decade since that cardigan's debut, Joji has continued taking bold steps. Her vision has unfolded in hundreds of designs, made by thousands of knitters, each one fueled by curiosity, unrestrained by convention. To complement the knits, she has also expanded her enterprise to include leather bags and accessories designed with the particular needs of knitters in mind.

Behind it all is a person of genuine grace. From her home in Buenos Aires, Joji has traveled the globe both virtually and in person, and she shares her designs and her generous worldview in a busy feed of photos and stories on social media.

In this Field Guide, you'll find a succinct collection of four slightly fancy knits that Joji designed for those times when we want to dress up just a bit.

Cuatro Wrap. Modular knitting at its best. Four graphic triangles, joined almost invisibly into a lavish stole that looks much more complicated to knit than it is.

Grace Notes Pullover. Embellished yet understated, full of signature Joji moments, this sweet sweater is simultaneously chic and cozy.

Gossamer. An ingenious swath of stockinette that can be worn as a vest or tossed over your shoulders like a scarf.

Fancy Beanie. This elevated topper is what happens when you let an unusually fuzzy yarn work its magic on simple stranded colorwork.

Our theme is grace, and our hope is that these knits will add grace notes to your knitting and your life.

Love,

Kay   Ann

CUATRO WRAP

Design by
Joji Locatelli

JOJI LOVES a big wrap, and so do we. The details are everything.

Structure. Four triangles, four colors, combined to create a parallelogram shape. Each triangle is worked separately, making this the sort of portable knitting that we really like. When the triangles are done, immerse yourself in the knitterly magic of grafting them together—the result is an elegant zigzag.

Color. Strong contrast is the name of the game here, graphic and sleek. The four colors each get a turn as the focus of a triangle.

Texture. This is mostly a stockinette project, but the occasional garter ridge adds a quiet element of texture.

Pattern. Stripes! We are eternally Team Stripes, especially when they combine in such playful ways.

There's something glorious about a swath of color, texture, and pattern, especially when it's in a yarn with good drape and a luxurious feel. Shown here is Woolfolk Tov DK, the softest merino we've ever seen, sometimes mistaken for cashmere.

KNITTED MEASUREMENTS

18" wide × 104" long [45.5 cm × 264 cm]

MATERIALS

— TOV DK by Woolfolk [50g skeins, each approx 160 yds (146 m), 100% Ovis 21 Ultimate Merino wool]: 2 skeins each #00 off-white (A), #2 medium gray (B), #3 dark gray (C), and #15 black (D)
— Size US 8 (5 mm) circular needle, 32" (80 cm) long, or size needed to obtain gauge
— Spare size US 8 (5 mm) or smaller circular needle, 32" (80 cm) long, for finishing
— Stitch markers
— 7 stitch holders or waste yarn

GAUGE

17.5 sts and 30 rows = 4" (10 cm) over stockinette stitch, after blocking

SPECIAL TECHNIQUE

Kitchener Stitch:

— Using a blunt tapestry needle, thread a length of yarn approximately 4 times the length of the section to be joined.
— With stitches still on the needles, hold the pieces to be joined parallel, with WSs together, both needle tips pointing to the right. Working from right to left:

Setup

— Insert tapestry needle into first stitch on front needle purlwise, pull yarn through, leaving stitch on needle.
— Insert tapestry needle into first stitch on back needle knitwise, pull yarn through, leaving stitch on needle.

Repeat for all stitches

— *Insert tapestry needle into first stitch on front needle knitwise, pull yarn through, remove stitch from needle.
— Insert tapestry needle into next stitch on front needle purlwise, pull yarn through, leave stitch on needle.
— Insert tapestry needle into first stitch on back needle purlwise, pull yarn through, remove stitch from needle.
— Insert tapestry needle into next stitch on back needle knitwise, pull yarn through, leave stitch on needle.
— Repeat from *, adjusting stitch tension every 3 or 4 stitches to match the pieces being joined.
— When 1 stitch remains on each needle, cut yarn and pass through last 2 stitches to fasten off.

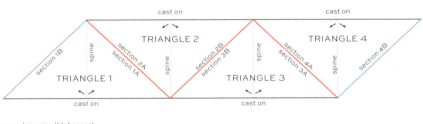

cast on

cast on

TRIANGLE 2

TRIANGLE 4

section 1B

spine

section 2A
section 1A

spine

section 2B
section 3B

spine

section 4A
section 3A

spine

section 4B

TRIANGLE 1

TRIANGLE 3

cast on

cast on

— Join using Kitchener st

— Bind off during finishing

NOTES

Wrap consists of 4 triangles worked separately, then joined together using Kitchener st. Each triangle is worked the same but with different colors. You'll increase 4 sts every RS row until triangle is complete. You'll work in st st or garter st, per Triangle Table on page 11.

If you have enough circular needles the same size as the working needle, or 1 size smaller, you can transfer the sts at the end of each triangle to spare circular needles instead of st holders or waste yarn. That way you won't have to transfer the sts back onto the needle to work Kitchener st.

TRIANGLE 1

— Using A, CO 3 sts.
— Knit 6 rows.
— Rotate piece 90° clockwise; pick up and knit 3 sts along side edge (1 st in each purl bump along edge); rotate piece 90° clockwise again; pick up and knit 3 sts across CO edge—9 sts.
— *Set-Up Row (WS)*: Sl 1, k1, p2, pm, p1 (spine st), pm, p2, k2.
— Using Triangle Table, work each section following number of rows given in color and st pattern listed. Work st patterns as follows:
To work in st st:
— *RS Row*: Sl 1, k1, M1R, knit to marker, M1R, sm, k1 (spine st), sm, M1L, knit to last 2 sts, M1L, k2—4 sts inc.
— *WS Row*: Sl 1, k1, purl to last 2 sts, k2.
To work in garter st:
— *RS Row*: Sl 1, k1, M1R, knit to marker, M1R, sm, k1 (spine st), sm, M1L, knit to last 2 sts, M1L, k2—4 sts inc.
— *WS Row*: Sl 1, knit to end.
— Continue until Triangle Table is complete—241 sts. Cut yarn and transfer first 121 sts (up to 2nd marker) to first st holder, removing markers (section 1A); transfer rem 120 sts to 2nd st holder (section 1B).

TRIANGLE 2

Work as for triangle 1, using B instead of A and C instead of B. Transfer sts to separate st holders (sections 2A and 2B).

TRIANGLE 3

Work as for triangle 1, using C instead of A and D instead of B. Transfer sts to separate st holders (sections 3A and 3B).

TRIANGLE 4

Work as for triangle 1, using D instead of A and A instead of B. Transfer sts to separate st holders (sections 4A and 4B).

FINISHING

— Cut a 60" (150 cm) long strand of B. Place sts from sections 1A and 2A onto 2 different circular needles. With WSs together, join sections using Kitchener st.
— Using C, rep for sections 2B and 3B.
— Using D, rep for sections 3A and 4A.
— Place sts from section 1B onto needle. With RS facing, using A, BO all sts knitwise.
— Using D, rep for section 4B.
— Weave in ends, closing any gaps at the joins; block as desired.

TRIANGLE TABLE

First Row of Section	Last Row of Section	Rows in Section	Increase (RS) Rows in Section	Color	Stitch Pattern	Total Stitches at End of Section
1	6	6	3	A	st st	21
7	8	2	1	A	garter st	25
9	14	6	3	A	st st	37
15	16	2	1	A	garter st	41
17	18	2	1	A	st st	45
19	20	2	1	B	st st	49
21	22	2	1	A	st st	53
23	24	2	1	B	st st	57
25	26	2	1	A	st st	61
27	28	2	1	A	garter st	65
29	34	6	3	A	st st	77
35	36	2	1	A	garter st	81
37	42	6	3	A	st st	93
43	44	2	1	A	garter st	97
45	46	2	1	A	st st	101
47	48	2	1	B	st st	105
49	50	2	1	A	st st	109
51	52	2	1	B	st st	113
53	54	2	1	A	st st	117
55	56	2	1	A	garter st	121
57	62	6	3	A	st st	133
63	64	2	1	A	garter st	137
65	70	6	3	A	st st	149
71	82	12	6	A	garter st	173
83	94	12	6	B	garter st	197
95	96	2	1	A	st st	201
97	98	2	1	B	st st	205
99	100	2	1	A	st st	209
101	102	2	1	B	st st	213
103	104	2	1	A	st st	217
105	116	12	6	A	garter st	241

GRACE NOTES PULLOVER

Design by
Joji Locatelli

L ISTENING TO JOJI talk about this project reminded us of the thoughtful approach she takes with all of her design work. Her aim here was to give us a slightly boxy pullover with appeal to the most knitters possible.

The construction is cool. The back is worked flat from the top down to the underarms. Then, making our way from the shoulder downward, the right and left sides are worked in turn, down to the point that we join them with the back to knit in the round to the hem. Sleeves come next, worked in the round, and the neckline is the final detail.

Along the way, Joji gives us twisted stitches inside the cables, twisted ribbing for the edgings, and a slim, tapered sleeve. These are all exquisite Joji details, grace notes for knitters. She loved using MDK Atlas yarn for this project. She said, and we quote, "It's a perfect yarn for this pullover." Music to our ears.

FINISHED MEASUREMENTS

Bust: 40 (44, 48, 52) (56, 60, 64) (68, 72, 76)" [101.5 (112, 122, 132) (142, 152.5, 162.5) (172.5, 183, 193) cm]

Length: 20.5 (21, 21.25, 21.5) (21.75, 22, 22.5) (23, 23.5, 23.5)" [52 (53.5, 54, 54.5) (55, 56, 57) (58.5, 59.5, 59.5) cm]

SIZES

To fit bust bust sizes 30-32 (34-36, 38-40, 42-44) (46-48, 50-52, 54-56) (58-60, 62-64, 66-68)" [76-81.5 (86.5-91.5, 96.5-101.5, 106.5-112) (117-122, 127-132, 137-142) (147.5-152.5, 157.5-162.5, 167.5-172.5) cm]

MATERIALS

— Atlas by Modern Daily Knitting [2 oz (57 g) skeins, each approx 145 yds (132.5 m), 100% Rambouillet wool]: 8 (8, 9, 10) (11, 11, 12) (13, 14, 14) skeins Pebble or Skyline
  Note: If lengthening the sleeves or body, you may need more yarn.

— Size US 6 (4 mm) circular needle, 16" (40 cm) and 24" (60 cm) long, and double-pointed needles (set of 4 or 5)

— Size US 7 (4.5 mm) circular needle, 32" (80 cm) long, and double-pointed needles (set of 4 or 5), or

size needed to achieve gauge

— Stitch markers
— Removable stitch marker
— Stitch holders or waste yarn
— Cable needle

GAUGE

20 sts and 28 rows = 4" (10 cm) over stockinette stitch using larger needle, after blocking

SPECIAL ABBREVIATIONS

6/6 LC (6 over 6 Left Cross): Slip the next 6 stitches to cable needle and hold at front of work, [p1, k1-tbl] 3 times, [p1, k1-tbl] 3 times from cable needle.

6/6 RC (6 over 6 Right Cross): Slip the next 6 stitches to cable needle and hold at back of work, [k1-tbl, p1] 3 times, [k1-tbl, p1] 3 times from cable needle.

S2kp2: Slip the next 2 stitches to right needle together as if to knit 2 together, knit 1 stitch, pass 2 slipped stitches over. Two stitches have been decreased.

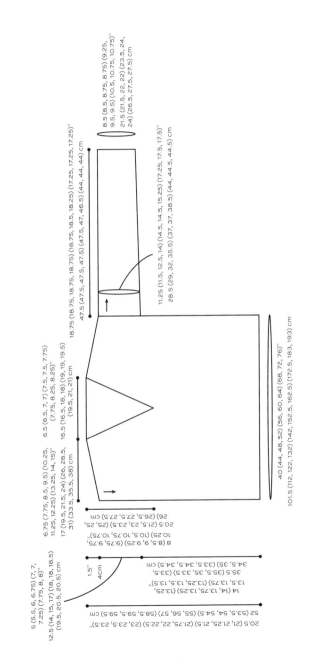

8.5 (8.5, 8.75, 8.75) (9.25, 9.5, 9.5) (10.5, 10.75, 10.75)"
21.5 (21.5, 22, 22) (23.5, 24, 24) (26.5, 27.5, 27.5) cm

18.75 (18.75, 18.75, 18.75) (18.75, 18.5, 18.25) (17.25, 17.25, 17.25)"
47.5 (47.5, 47.5, 47.5) (47.5, 47, 46.5) (44, 44, 44) cm

11.25 (11.5, 12.5, 14) (14.5, 14.5, 15.25) (17.25, 17.5, 17.5)"
28.5 (29, 32, 35.5) (37, 37, 38.5) (44, 44.5, 44.5) cm

6.75 (7.75, 8.5, 9.5) (10.25, 11.25, 12.25) (13.25, 14, 15)"
17 (19.5, 21.5, 24) (26, 28.5, 31) (33.5, 35.5, 38) cm

6.5 (6.5, 7, 7) (7.5, 7.5, 7.75) (7.75, 8.25, 8.25)"
16.5 (16.5, 18, 18) (19, 19, 19.5) (19.5, 21, 21) cm

40 (44, 48, 52) (56, 60, 64) (68, 72, 76)"
101.5 (112, 122, 132) (142, 152.5, 162.5) (172.5, 183, 193) cm

8 (8.5, 9, 9.25) (9.75, 9.75, 10.25) (10.5, 10.75, 10.75)"
20.5 (21.5, 23, 23.5) (25, 25, 26) (26.5, 27.5, 27.5) cm

1.5"
4cm

14 (14, 13.75, 13.25) (13.25, 13.5, 13.5) (13.5, 13.75, 13.75)"
34.5, 35) (35, 35.5, 35, 33.5) (33.5, 34.5, 34.5) cm

20.5 (21, 21.25, 21.5) (21.75, 22, 22.5) (23, 23.5, 23.5)"
52 (53.5, 54, 54.5) (55, 56, 57) (58.5, 59.5, 59.5) cm

5 (5.5, 6, 6.75) (7, 7, 7.25) (7.75, 8, 8)"
12.5 (14, 15, 17) (18, 18, 18.5) (19.5, 20.5, 20.5) cm

TWISTED RIB

(odd number of sts)

All Rnds: K1-tbl, *p1, k1-tbl; rep from
* to end.

TWISTED RIB

(even number of sts)

All Rnds: *K1-tbl, p1; rep from * to end.

FLAT LEFT CABLE

(panel of 21 sts)

— *Row 1 (RS)*: P1, [k1-tbl, p1] 10 times.
— *Row 2*: K1, [p1-tbl, k1] 10 times.
— *Rows 3 and 4*: Rep Rows 1 and 2.
— *Row 5*: [P1, k1-tbl] twice, 6/6 LC, p1, [k1-tbl, p1] twice.
— *Row 6*: Rep Row 2.
— *Rows 7–12*: Rep Rows 3 and 4 three times.
— Repeat Rows 1–12 for Flat Left Cable.

CIRCULAR LEFT CABLE

(panel of 21 sts)

— *Rnd 1–4*: P1, [k1-tbl, p1] 10 times.
— *Rnd 5*: [P1, k1-tbl] twice, 6/6 LC, p1, [k1-tbl, p1] twice.
— *Rnds 6–12*: P1, [k1-tbl, p1] 10 times.
— Repeat Rnds 1–12 for Circular Left Cable.

FLAT RIGHT CABLE

(panel of 21 sts)

— *Row 1 (RS)*: P1, [k1-tbl, p1] 10 times.
— *Row 2*: K1, [p1-tbl, k1] 10 times.
— *Rows 3 and 4*: Rep Rows 1 and 2.
— *Row 5*: P1, [k1-tbl, p1] twice, 6/6 RC, [k1-tbl, p1] twice.
— *Row 6*: Rep Row 2.
— *Rows 7–12*: Rep Rows 3 and 4 three times.
— Repeat Rows 1–12 for Flat Right Cable.

CIRCULAR RIGHT CABLE

(panel of 21 sts)

— *Rnd 1–4*: P1, [k1-tbl, p1] 10 times.
— *Rnd 5*: P1, [k1-tbl, p1] twice, 6/6 RC, [k1-tbl, p1] twice.
— *Rnds 6–12*: P1, [k1-tbl, p1] 10 times.
— Repeat Rnds 1–12 for Circular Right Cable.

SPECIAL TECHNIQUE

Wrap-and-Turn Short Rows: Short-row shaping allows you to work extra rows on a particular section of your knitting, such as the back neck, without adding rows to the entire piece. Work short rows using w&t as instructed, then work wraps together with wrapped sts as you come to them, as follows: If

working on a knit st, insert right needle into the wrap from below, then into wrapped st and knit them together. If working on a purl st, lift back leg of wrap onto left needle, then work it together with wrapped st. When working short rows across rib pattern, you may leave wraps in place rather than working them together with wrapped sts as the ribbing will hide them.

NOTES

Pullover is worked from the top down. The back is worked to the underarms, with short-row shoulder shaping. The fronts are picked up separately from the shoulders and worked to the underarms, with short-row shoulder shaping. The back and fronts are joined and worked to the end of the neck shaping. The fronts are joined and the body is worked in the round to the hem. Stitches are picked up from the armholes for the sleeves and worked in the round to the hem.

The length of the body and sleeves is adjustable. Compare the schematic lengths to your favorite sweater and adjust the lengths accordingly. Keep in mind that if you lengthen the sweater, you may need additional yarn.

BACK

— Using larger needle, CO 109 (119, 129, 139) (149, 159, 169) (179, 189, 199) sts.

— *Set-Up Row (RS)*: K17 (22, 26, 31) (35, 40, 44) (49, 53, 58), pm, p1, [k1-tbl, p1] 10 times, pm, k33 (33, 35, 35) (37, 37, 39) (39, 41, 41), pm, p1, [k1-tbl, p1] 10 times, pm, k17 (22, 26, 31) (35, 40, 44) (49, 53, 58).

SHAPE SHOULDERS

— *Short Row 1 (WS)*: Purl to marker, sm, k1, *p1-tbl, k1; rep from * to marker, sm, purl to marker, sm, [k1, p1-tbl] twice, w&t.

— *Short Row 2*: [K1-tbl, p1] twice, sm, knit to marker, sm, [p1, k1-tbl] twice, w&t.

— *Short Row 3*: [P1-tbl, k1] twice, sm, purl to marker, sm, [k1, p1-tbl] 6 times, w&t.

— *Short Row 4*: *K1-tbl, p1; rep from * to marker, sm, knit to marker, sm, [p1, k1-tbl] 6 times, w&t.

— *Short Row 5*: *P1-tbl, k1; rep from * to marker, sm, purl to marker, sm, [k1, p1-tbl] 10 times, w&t.

— *Short Row 6*: *K1-tbl, p1; rep from * to marker, sm, knit to marker, sm, [p1, k1-tbl] 10 times, w&t.

— *Short Row 7*: *P1-tbl, k1; rep from * to marker, sm, purl to marker, sm, k1, **p1-tbl, k1; rep from ** to marker, sm, p5 (7, 8, 10) (11, 13, 14) (15, 16, 18), w&t.

— *Short Row 8 (RS)*: Knit to marker, sm, work Row 1 of Flat Left Cable to marker, sm, knit to marker, sm, work Row 1 of Flat Right Cable to marker, sm, k5 (7, 8, 10) (11, 13, 14) (15, 16, 18), w&t.

— *Short Row 9*: Purl to marker, sm, work next row of Flat Right Cable to marker, sm, purl to marker, sm, work next row of Flat Left Cable to marker, sm, purl to 5 (7, 8, 10) (11, 13, 14) (15, 16, 18) sts after wrapped st from previous WS row, w&t.

— *Short Row 10*: Knit to marker, sm, work to last marker, sm, knit to 5 (7, 8, 10) (11, 13, 14) (15, 16, 18) sts after wrapped st of previous RS row, w&t.

— *Short Row 11*: Purl to marker, sm, work to last marker, sm, purl to end.

— *Row 12*: Knit to marker, sm, work to last marker, sm, knit to end.

— Work until armholes measure 5.25 (5.5, 6, 6.75) (7, 7, 7.25) (8.25, 8.5, 8.5)" [13.5 (14, 15, 17) (18, 18, 18.5) (21, 21.5, 21.5) cm] (measured along edges), ending with WS row. Record last row worked. Cut yarn; put sts on holder.

— Place removable markers 38 (43, 47, 52) (56, 61, 65) (70, 74, 79) sts in from each edge on CO row.

RIGHT FRONT

With RS of back facing, using larger needle and beg at right armhole edge, pick up and knit 38 (43, 47, 52) (56, 61, 65) (70, 74, 79) sts along back CO edge between right armhole edge and first marker.

SHAPE SHOULDER AND NECK

— *Short Row 1 (WS)*: [K1, p1-tbl] twice, w&t.
— *Short Row 2*: *K1-tbl, p1; rep from * to end.
— *Short Row 3*: [K1, p1-tbl] 6 times, w&t.
— *Short Row 4*: Rep Short Row 2.
— *Short Row 5*: [K1, p1-tbl] 10 times, w&t.
— *Short Row 6*: Rep Short Row 2.
— *Short Row 7*: [K1, p1-tbl] 10 times, k1, pm, p5 (7, 8, 10) (11, 13, 14) (15, 16, 18), w&t.
— *Short Row 8*: Knit to marker, sm, work Row 1 of Flat Left Cable to end.
— *Short Row 9*: Work next row of Flat Left Cable to marker, sm, purl to 5 (7, 8, 10) (11, 13, 14) (15, 16, 18) sts after wrapped st of previous WS row, w&t.

— *Short Row 10*: Knit to marker, M1L, sm, work to end—1 st inc.
— *Row 11*: Work to marker, sm, purl to end.
— *Row 12*: Knit to marker, sm, work to end.
— *Row 13*: Work to marker, sm, purl to end.

SHAPE NECK

— *Inc Row (RS)*: Knit to marker, M1L, sm, work to end—1 st inc.
— Rep Inc Row every 4 rows 7 (8, 9, 10) (11, 11, 11) (12, 12, 12) times, then every RS row 1 (0, 0, 1) (0, 0, 0) (0, 1, 1) time(s)—48 (53, 58, 65) (69, 74, 78) (84, 89, 94) sts.
— Work even until armhole measures 5.25 (5.5, 6, 6.75) (7, 7, 7.25) (8.25, 8.5, 8.5)" [13.5 (14, 15, 17) (18, 18, 18.5) (21, 21.5, 21.5) cm] from pick-up row, measured along armhole edge, ending with same row of Left Cable as for back. Cut yarn and place sts on st holder or waste yarn.

LEFT FRONT

— With RS of back facing you, using larger needle and beg at 2nd marker, pick up and knit 38 (43, 47, 52) (56, 61, 65) (70, 74, 79) sts along back

CO edge between 2nd marker and left armhole edge.

— *Set-Up Row (WS)*: P17 (22, 26, 31) (35, 40, 44, 49, 53, 58), pm, k1, *p1-tbl, k1; rep from * to end.

SHAPE SHOULDER AND NECK

— *Short Row 1 (RS)*: [P1, k1-tbl] twice, w&t.
— *Short Row 2*: *K1, p1-tbl; rep from * to end.
— *Short Row 3*: [P1, k1-tbl] 6 times, w&t.
— *Short Row 4*: Rep Short Row 2.
— Short Row 5: [P1, k1-tbl] 10 times, w&t.
— *Short Row 6*: Rep Short Row 2.
— *Short Row 7*: Work Row 1 of Flat Right Cable to marker, sm, k5 (7, 8, 10) (11, 13, 14) (15, 16, 18), w&t.
— *Short Row 8*: Purl to marker, sm, work next row of Flat Right Cable to end.
— *Short Row 9*: Work to marker, sm, M1R, knit to 5 (7, 8, 10) (11, 13, 14) (15, 16, 18) sts after wrapped st from previous RS row, w&t—1 st inc.
— *Short Row 10*: Rep Short Row 8.
— *Row 11*: Work to marker, sm, knit to end.
— *Row 12*: Purl to marker, sm, work to end.

SHAPE NECK

— *Inc Row (RS)*: Work to marker, sm, M1R, knit to end—1 st inc.
— Rep Inc Row every 4 rows 7 (8, 9, 10) (11, 11, 11) (12, 12, 12) times, then every RS row 1 (0, 0, 1) (0, 0, 0) (0, 1, 1) time(s)—48 (53, 58, 65) (69, 74, 78) (84, 89, 94) sts.
— Work even until armhole measures 5.25 (5.5, 6, 6.75) (7, 7, 7.25) (8.25, 8.5, 8.5)" [13.5 (14, 15, 17) (18, 18, 18.5) (21, 21.5, 21.5) cm] from pick-up row, measured along armhole edge, ending with same row of Right Cable as for back.

BODY

JOIN FRONTS AND BACK

Joining Row (RS): With yarn attached to left front, work to marker, sm, M1R, knit to end of left front; work in established patterns across back, pm; working across right front sts, knit to marker, M1L, sm, work to end of right front; do not join—207 (227, 247, 271) (289, 309, 327) (349, 369, 389) sts.

CONTINUE NECK SHAPING

— *Next Row (WS)*: Work to marker, sm, [purl to marker, sm] twice, work to marker, sm, purl to marker, sm, work to marker, sm, purl to marker, sm, work to end.

— *Inc Row (RS)*: Work to marker, sm, M1R, work to last marker, M1L, sm, work to end—2 sts inc.

— Rep Inc Row every RS row 4 (4, 4, 2) (3, 3, 4) (3, 3, 3) more times, ending with a WS row—217 (237, 257, 277) (297, 317, 337) (357, 377, 397) sts; 54 (59, 64, 69) (74, 79, 84) (89, 94, 99) sts each front, and 109 (119, 129, 139) (149, 159, 169) (179, 189, 199) sts for back.

— Cut yarn. With RS facing, transfer 54 (59, 64, 69) (74, 79, 84) (89, 94, 99) right front sts to left needle, in front of left front sts. Join yarn, ready to work a RS row across right front sts. The right side marker is now new beg-of-rnd marker.

JOIN BODY

Note: Change to Circular Right and Left Cables, beginning with rnd following last row worked in Flat Right and Left Cables.

— *Rnd 1*: Work to end of right front sts, pm, M1L (center front st), work to end of rnd—218 (238, 258, 278) (298, 318, 338) (358, 378, 398) sts.

— *Rnd 2*: Work to 2nd marker, remove marker, k1-tbl, work to end.

— Work even in established patterns, working center front st as k1-tbl, until piece measures 11.5 (11.5, 11.25, 10.75) (10.75, 11, 11.25) (10.75, 11, 11)" [29 (29, 28.5, 27.5) (27.5, 28, 28.5) (27.5, 28, 28) cm] from underarm or to 2.5" [6.5 cm] less than desired length, ending final rnd at last marker before beg-of-rnd marker (now new beg-of-rnd marker).

— *Set-Up Rnd*: [K2tog] 1 (1, 0, 0) (1, 1, 0) (0, 1, 1) time(s), knit to former beg-of-rnd marker (remove marker), knit to marker, sm, work to marker, sm, [k2tog] 1 (1, 0, 0) (1, 1, 0) (0, 1, 1) time(s), work to end—216 (236, 258, 278) (296, 316, 338) (358, 376, 396) sts.

RIBBING

— *Rnd 1*: Work Twisted Rib to marker, sm, [work in established pattern to marker, sm] twice, *work Twisted Rib to marker, sm, work in established pattern to marker, sm; rep from * once more.

— Repeat Rnd 1 for 2.5" [6.5 cm]. BO all sts in pattern.

SLEEVES

— With RS facing, using larger dpns and beg at center underarm, pick up and knit 56 (58, 62, 70) (72, 72, 76) (86, 88, 88) sts evenly around armhole. Join; pm for beg of rnd and work in the rnd as follows:

— Beg st st (knit every rnd); work 14 rnds even.

SHAPE SLEEVE

— *Dec Rnd*: K1, ssk, knit to last 3 sts, k2tog, k1—2 sts dec.

— Rep Dec Rnd every 16 (14, 12, 8) (8, 8, 8) (6, 6, 6) rnds 1 (1, 3, 7) (7, 9, 3) (6, 6, 6) more time(s), then every 14 (12, 10, 6) (6, 6, 6) (4, 4, 4) rnds 5 (6, 5, 5) (5, 2, 10) (10, 10, 10) times—42 (42, 44, 44) (46, 48, 48) (52, 54, 54) sts.

— Work even until piece measures 16 (16, 16, 16) (16, 15.75, 15.5) (14.5, 14.5, 14.5)" [40.5 (40.5, 40.5, 40.5) (40.5, 40, 39.5) (37, 37, 37) cm] from pick-up rnd, or 2.75" [7 cm] less than your desired length.

— Change to smaller dpns. Work in Twisted Rib for 2.75" [7 cm].

— BO all sts in pattern.

NECKBAND

— With RS facing, using smaller 16" (40 cm) circular needle and beginning at right shoulder seam, pick up and knit 33 (33, 35, 35) (37, 37, 39) (39, 41, 41) sts along back neck edge, 41 (43, 45, 45) (47, 47, 51) (53, 55, 55) sts along left front neck edge to center front, 1 st in center (place removable marker around this st), then 41 (43, 45, 45) (47, 47, 51) (53, 55, 55) sts along right front neck edge—116 (120, 126, 126) (132, 132, 142) (146, 152, 152) sts. Join; pm for beg of rnd and work in the rnd as follows:

— Rnd 1: K1-tbl, *p1, k1-tbl; rep from * to 1 st before marked center st, s2kp2, **k1-tbl, p1; rep from ** to end—2 sts dec.

— Rnd 2: *K1-tbl, p1; rep from * to 1 st before marked center st, s2kp2, p1, **k1-tbl, p1; rep from ** to end—2 sts dec.

— Rep Rnd 1 once more—2 sts dec.

— BO all sts in pattern, working s2kp2 at center front neck as you BO.

FINISHING

Weave in ends; block as desired.

JOJI & CO

WHEN JOJI LOCATELLI announced her new line of bags, Joji & Co., we were instantly curious. What leads a knitwear designer to get into the bag business?

Joji explains: "On date nights and for dinners with friends, I love to dress up. That doesn't mean I am leaving my knitting behind: NEVER! I wanted classic and elegant bags that would go with a nice outfit."

Yes! Exactly! Sometimes we want to class it up.

Living in Argentina, with its long tradition of beautiful leather-working, Joji realized that she could work with local artisans to create the bags of her dreams. Beginning with black and yellow, her favorite non-color and color, she has grown her offerings to include more sizes, more colors, more features.

Here at MDK we tend to keep track of our projects by dedicating a bag to each one. Maybe this is a bit much, but we don't think so. The perfect project requires the perfect container, and Joji's elegant Recoleta Bag—named after the French quarter in Buenos Aires—sets us up for glory.

GOSSAMER

Design by
Joji Locatelli

IN DESIGNING this inventive garment, Joji was inspired by the ruana, a traditional cape with roots in Colombia and Venezuela. Where the classic ruana is rugged and enveloping, Joji's iteration is so delicate it practically floats. The secret is a double strand of Kidsilk Haze, a laceweight blend of silk and mohair, fibers prized for their elegance, luminosity, and insulating properties.

A long rectangle that is split, this design is convertible: it can be styled like a vest as shown here, with the two narrow pieces in the front and the wide half down the back, held in place by buttons down the front and sides.

But this versatile piece can also be folded the long way, and wrapped around the neck and shoulders, with the shell buttons now just there for sparkle and heft (see page 33). It's the perfect piece to slip into your bag in case of a chill, or a call for an instant glamor upgrade.

KNITTED MEASUREMENTS

Bust: 37 (40, 44, 48) (52, 56, 59) (63, 67, 71)" [94 (101.5, 112, 122) (132, 142, 150) (160, 170, 180.5) cm]

Length: 25.25 (25.25, 26, 26.5) (27.5, 28, 29.25) (29.5, 30, 31.25)" [64 (64, 66, 67.5) (70, 71, 74.5) (75, 76, 79.5) cm]

Length when worn as a wrap: 50.5 (50.5, 52, 53) (55, 56, 58.5) (59, 60, 62.5)" [128.5 (128.5, 132, 134.5) (139.5, 142, 148.5) (150, 152.5, 159) cm]

SIZES

To fit bust sizes 30-32 (34-36, 38-40, 42-44) (46-48, 50-52, 54-56) (58-60, 62-64, 66-68)" [76-81.5 (86.5-91.5, 96.5-101.5, 106.5-112) (117-122, 127-132, 137-142) (147.5-152.5, 157.5-162.5, 167.5-172.5) cm]

MATERIALS

— Kidsilk Haze by Rowan [25g balls, each approx 229 yds (210 m), 70% mohair, 30% silk]: 5 (6, 6, 7) (8, 9, 9) (10, 11, 12) balls #605 Smoke
— Size US 7 (4.5 mm) circular needle, 32" (80 cm) long, or size needed to obtain gauge
— Stitch markers
— Stitch holders
— Twelve ⅜" (1 cm) buttons (to keep this design as versatile as possible,

we recommend picking buttons that have a low profile and a color as close as possible to your yarn color. Joji's preference is for mother of pearl buttons or something similar.)

GAUGE

17 sts and 24 rows = 4" (10 cm) over stockinette stitch, using 2 strands of yarn held together, after blocking

2×2 RIB

(multiple of 4 sts + 2)
— *Row 1 (RS)*: Sl 1, k1, *p2, k2; rep from * to end.
— *Row 2*: Sl 1, p1, *k2, p2; rep from * to end.
— Rep Rows 1 and 2 for 2×2 Rib.

NOTE

This garment is worked in one piece from the bottom edge of the back, over the shoulders where the fronts are divided and worked separately, to the bottom hem.

9.25 (10, 11, 12) (13, 14, 14.75)
(15.75, 16.75, 17.75)"

23.5 (25.5, 28, 30.5) (33,
35.5, 37.5) (40, 42.5, 45) cm

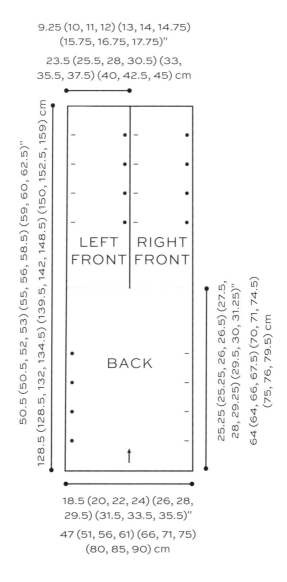

50.5 (50.5, 52, 53) (55, 56, 58.5) (59, 60, 62.5)"

128.5 (128.5, 132, 134.5) (139.5, 142, 148.5) (150, 152.5, 159) cm

LEFT FRONT

RIGHT FRONT

BACK

25.25 (25.25, 26, 26.5) (27.5, 28, 29.25) (29.5, 30, 31.25)"

64 (64, 66, 67.5) (70, 71, 74.5) (75, 76, 79.5) cm

18.5 (20, 22, 24) (26, 28,
29.5) (31.5, 33.5, 35.5)"

47 (51, 56, 61) (66, 71, 75)
(80, 85, 90) cm

BACK

— Using 2 strands of yarn held together, CO 78 (86, 94, 102) (110, 118, 126) (134, 142, 150) sts.
— Beg 2×2 Rib; work even until piece measures 3.5" (9 cm).
— *Row 1 (RS)*: Sl 1, p1, [k1, p1] 3 times, pm, k29 (33, 37, 41) (45, 49, 53) (57, 61, 65), pm, p1, k2, p1, pm, k29 (33, 37, 41) (45, 49, 53) (57, 61, 65), pm, *p1, k1; rep from * to end.
— *Row 2*: Sl 1, k1, *p1, k1; rep from * to marker, sm, purl to marker, sm, k1, sl 2 wyif, k1, sm, purl to marker, sm, **k1, p1; rep from ** to end.
— *Row 3*: Sl 1, p1, *k1, p1; rep from * to marker, sm, knit to marker, sm, p1, k2, p1, sm, knit to marker, sm, **p1, k1; rep from ** to end.
— Rep Row 2.
— *Buttonhole Row 1 (RS)*: Sl 1, p1, yo, ssk, [k1, p1] twice, sm, knit to marker, sm, p1, k2, p1, sm, knit to marker, sm, *p1, k1; rep from * to end.
— Work even, working Buttonhole Row 1 on RS rows every 4" (10 cm) 3 more times, then work even until piece measures 25.25 (25.25, 26, 26.5) (27.5, 28, 29.25) (29.5, 30, 31.25)" [64 (64, 66, 67.5) (70, 71, 74.5) (75, 76, 79.5) cm, ending with a WS row.

DIVIDE FOR FRONTS

— *Division Row (RS)*: Sl 1, p1, *k1, p1; rep from * to marker, sm, knit to 6 sts before marker, pm, [p1, k1] 3 times, remove marker, p1, k1, transfer the last 39 (43, 47, 51) (55, 59, 63) (67, 71, 75) sts worked to st holder or waste yarn for right front, k1, p1, remove marker, [k1, p1] 3 times, pm, knit to marker, sm, **p1, k1; rep from ** to end—39 (43, 47, 51) (55, 59, 63) (67, 71, 75) sts for left front.

LEFT FRONT

— *Next Row (WS)*: Sl 1, k1, *p1, k1; rep from * to marker, sm, purl to marker, sm, **k1, p1; rep from ** to end.
— *Next Row*: Sl 1, p1, *k1, p1; rep from * to marker, sm, knit to marker, sm, **p1, k1; rep from ** to end.
— Work even until piece measures 9.25 (9.25, 10, 10.5) (11.5, 12, 13.25) (13.5, 14, 15.25)" [23.5 (23.5, 25.5, 26.5) (29, 30.5, 33.5) (34.5, 35.5, 38.5) cm] from divide, ending with a WS row.
— *Buttonhole Row 2 (RS)*: Sl 1, p1, *k1, p1; rep from * to marker, sm, knit to marker, sm, [p1, k1] twice, k2tog, yo, p1, k1.
— Work even, working Buttonhole

Row 2 on RS rows every 4" (10 cm) 3 more times.

— Work 3 rows even, or until left front measures same as back from shoulder to top of rib.

— *Set-Up Row (RS):* Sl 1, k1, p2tog, p1, k2, *p2, k2; rep from * to end—38 (42, 46, 50) (54, 58, 62) (66, 70, 74) sts remain.

— Beg 2×2 Rib; work 3.5" (9 cm) even.

— BO all sts in rib.

RIGHT FRONT

— With WS facing, rejoin yarn to right front sts. Work as for left front. The buttonholes will be on the neck edge of the right front and the armhole edge of the left front.

FINISHING

— Weave in ends; block as desired.

— Sew buttons opposite buttonholes on the left edge of the back, the neck edge of the left front, and the armhole edge of the right front.

FANCY
BEANIE

Design by
Joji Locatelli

SOMETIMES THE YARN does it all. In this case, the yarn is Neighborhood Fiber Company's Suri Loft, a luxurious blend of suri alpaca, merino, and silk. When the posh fuzz of Suri Loft is applied to a classic beanie and a simple 2×2 stranded colorwork pattern, the result is a softly blurred checkerboard hat. At a glance, it's hard to tell what's going on—but whatever it is, it's special. We want it.

KNITTED MEASUREMENTS

Circumference: 16.75 (20)" [42.5 (51) cm]
Length: 10.25 (10.75)" [26 (27.5) cm].

SIZES

Adult medium (large)
To fit head circumference 20-21.5 (22-24)" [51-54.5 (56-61) cm]

MATERIALS

— Suri Loft by Neighborhood Fiber Co.
  [50g skeins, each approx
  190 yds (174 m), 65% suri alpaca,
  20% merino, 15% silk]: 1 skein
  each MC and A
  Colorway 1: Charles Centre (MC),
  Thomas Circle (A)
  Colorway 2: Mondawmin (MC),
  Charles Centre (A)
— Size US 4 (3.5 mm) circular needle,
  16" (10 cm) long and double-pointed
  needles (set of 4 or 5), or size
  needed to achieve gauge
— Size US 2 (2.75 mm) circular needle,
  16" (10 cm) long
— Stitch marker

GAUGE

24 sts and 30 rows = 4" (10 cm) over
Checkerboard Pattern, using larger
needle, after blocking

CHECKERBOARD PATTERN

(multiple of 4 sts)

— *Rnds 1–3*: *With A k2, with MC k2;
  rep from * to end.
— *Rnds 4–6*: *With MC k2, with A k2;
  rep from * to end.
— Rep Rnds 1–6 for Checkerboard
  Pattern.

NOTE

You may work the Checkerboard Pattern
and crown shaping from either the text or
the charts.

Checkerboard Pattern

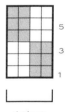

4-st rep

Crown Chart

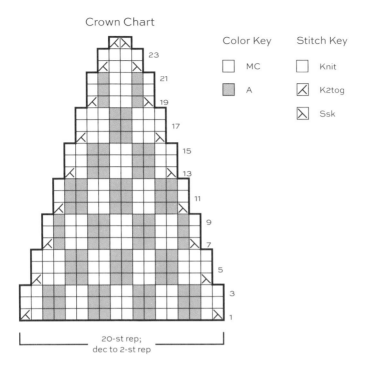

Color Key

☐ MC

▨ A

Stitch Key

☐ Knit

◺ K2tog

◿ Ssk

23
21
19
17
15
13
11
9
7
5
3
1

20-st rep;
dec to 2-st rep

BEANIE

— Using MC and smaller needle, CO 100 (120 sts). Join, being careful not to twist sts; pm for beg of rnd and work in the rnd as follows:

— *Rnd 1*: *K2, p2; rep from * to end.

— Rep Rnd 1 until piece measures 3 (3.5)" [7.5 (9) cm].

— Change to larger needle.

— Beg Checkerboard Pattern (working from text or chart); work even until piece measures 8 (8.5)" [20.5 (21.5) cm], ending with Rnd 5 of pattern.

— *Next Rnd*: Work Rnd 6 to end, remove beg-of-rnd marker, with MC k1; pm for new beg of rnd.

SHAPE CROWN

Notes: Change to dpns when necessary for number of sts on needle. You may work from the chart or the following text.

— *Rnd 1*: *With MC ssk, k1, [with A k2, with MC k2] 3 times, with A k2, with MC k1, k2tog; repeat from * to end—90 (108) sts remain.

- *Rnds 2 and 3*: *With MC k2, [with A k2, with MC k2] 4 times; repeat from * to end.
- *Rnd 4*: *With MC ssk, k2, [with A k2, with MC k2] 3 times, with MC k2tog; repeat from * to end—80 (96) sts remain.
- *Rnds 5 and 6*: *With MC k3, [with A k2, with MC k2] 3 times, with MC k1; repeat from * to end.
- *Rnd 7*: *With MC ssk, with A k1, [with MC k2, with A k2] twice, with MC k2, with A k1, with MC k2tog; repeat from *to end—70 (84) sts remain.
- *Rnds 8 and 9*: *With MC k1, with A k1, [with MC k2, with A k2] twice, with MC k2, with A k1, with MC k1; repeat from *to end.
- *Rnd 10*: *With MC ssk, [with A k2, with MC k2] twice, with A k2, with MC k2tog; repeat from * to end—60 (72) sts remain.
- *Rnds 11 and 12*: *With MC k1, [with A k2, with MC k2] twice, with A k2, with MC k1; repeat from * to end.
- *Rnd 13*: *With MC ssk, k1, with A k2, with MC k2, with A k2, with MC k1, k2tog; repeat from * to end—50 (64) sts remain.
- *Rnds 14 and 15*: *With MC k2, [with A k2, with MC k2] twice; repeat from * to end.
- *Rnd 16*: *With MC ssk, k2, with A k2, with MC k2, k2tog; repeat from * to end—40 (48) sts remain.
- *Rnds 17 and 18*: *With MC k3, with A k2, with MC k3; repeat from * to end.
- *Rnd 19*: *With MC ssk, with A k1, with MC k2, with A k1, with MC k2tog; repeat from * to end—30 (36) sts remain.
- *Rnds 20 and 21*: *With MC k1, with A k1, with MC k2, with A k1, with MC k1; repeat from * to end. Cut A.
- *Rnd 22*: *With MC, ssk, k2, k2tog; repeat from * to end—20 (24) sts remain.
- *Rnd 23*: Knit.
- *Rnd 24*: *Ssk, k2tog; repeat from * to end—10 (12) sts remain.
- Cut yarn, leaving a long tail. Thread tail through rem sts, pull tight and fasten off.

FINISHING
Weave in ends; block as desired, stretching the crown while blocking so it lies flat.

MEET JOJI LOCATELLI

As a child, Joji Locatelli learned to knit from her mother but she didn't imagine a career as a knitwear designer until many years later—after finishing medical school, working as a doctor for a couple of years, and starting a family.

What did you learn in medical school and while working as a doctor that serves you well in your career as a knitwear designer and entrepreneur?
Going to medical school was one of the happiest times of my life. That experience taught me to persevere, to see a goal and fight for it.

In my second year I was offered a job teaching anatomy, and I did that until I graduated. I learned to teach, to listen, to be understanding. I learned we all have different kinds of intelligence and ways of learning. It taught me to motivate my students to give their best. Now I love to encourage knitters to discover what they are able to achieve.

During school I also spent a lot of time learning about mental health and doctor-patient relationships. I learned how to make myself available and approachable to someone who's really in need of a word, or an ear. I know knitting is sometimes the only therapy for people who are going through tough times. I want my designs to bring knitters pleasure without causing any extra anxiety.

Do you feel that being a knitter plays a role in your health?
Definitely. For starters, I took up knitting as my therapy while trying to quit smoking. And it worked! I also rely on knitting to cope with hardship. It was my comfort blanket while dealing with loss of dear ones. It's my connection to my mother, it's my creative outlet as well as my work. I honestly think I am a much

more fabulous person ever since I became a knitter, like every knitter I know!

You learned to knit as a child like most Argentinians—by "reading" an existing garment and swatching and doing the math necessary to create it as is or with your own variations. What do you want to learn these days?

Recently I've been focusing on learning brioche stitch well enough to design with it. I'm also interested in mastering steeking and intarsia. For me, what works best is just to jump in, grab a pattern, and start a project that includes the skill I'm trying to learn and trust that the designer (or Google) will tell me what to do when the time comes.

We know you love to travel. How does travel influence you as a knitter and designer—and in life generally?

I am as serious about traveling and exploring as I am about knitting. I couldn't afford to travel anywhere until I was in my 30s, when I took my first trip abroad—to Europe—and it just blew my mind. The people, colors, food, culture. Everything felt different and exciting. I am a different person when I am abroad; I become the outsider, which is fun and intriguing.

I work so I can afford to travel. I don't care for expensive things, but traveling is expensive, so I am always very motivated.

Traveling gives me adventure. It shows me different ways to use my knitting knowledge. It connects me with crafters and materials from all over the world, and I am a much more colorful designer because of it (color as a metaphor, I still love to knit with just gray).

You were intentional about sticking mostly to black, gray, and natural for the samples in this Field Guide. What compelled you to make that choice?

I love color, but I also know we all experience color in different ways, so a color that I may find exciting, elegant, and cheerful, like yellow, might not translate the same way for others.

I feel like a grayscale palette lets everyone "see" the colors they want in designs. One person might imagine the Grace Notes Pullover in pink and plan ways to incorporate that into their wardrobe, while someone else might think of a completely different color. I love that lack of color actually prompts people to THINK about color.

ABBREVIATIONS

Approx: Approximately

Beg: Begin(ning)(s)

BO: Bind off

Cn: Cable needle

CO: Cast on

Dec: Decreas(ed)(es)(ing)

Dpn: Double-pointed needle(s)

Inc: Increas(ed)(es)(ing)

K: Knit

K2tog: Knit 2 stitches together. One stitch has been decreased.

M1L: (Make 1 left) Insert left needle from front to back under horizontal strand between stitch just worked and the next stitch on the left needle. Knit this strand through the back loop. One stitch has been increased.

M1R: (Make 1 right) Insert left needle from back to front under horizontal strand between stitch just worked and the next stitch on the left needle. Knit this strand through the front loop. One stitch has been increased.

P: Purl

P2tog: Purl 2 stitches together. One stitch has been decreased.

Pm: Place marker

Rep: Repeat(ed)(ing)(s)

Rnd(s): Round(s)

RS: Right side

Sl: Slip

Sm: Slip marker

Ssk: Slip 1 stitch knitwise, slip 1 stitch purlwise, insert left needle into the front of these 2 stitches and knit them together from this position. One stitch has been decreased.